Meghan

Has a Secret

written by
Lori Z. Scott

illustrated by
Stacy Curtis

Standard®
PUBLISHING

Cincinnati, Ohio

Published by Standard Publishing, Cincinnati, Ohio
www.standardpub.com

Printed in: USA
Project editor: Laura Derico
Cover and interior design: Holli Conger

ISBN 978-0-7847-2107-0

Library of Congress Cataloging-in-Publication Data

Scott, Lori Z., 1965-
  Meghan Rose has a secret / written by Lori Z. Scott;
illustrated by Stacy Curtis.
       p. cm.
  Summary: When Meghan Rose and her two best friends buy
diaries at the school book fair, Meghan learns about the power
of words to both hurt and heal. Includes discussion questions
and activities.
  ISBN 978-0-7847-2107-0 (perfect bound)
  [1. Diaries—Fiction. 2. Best friends—Fiction. 3. Friendship—
Fiction. 4. Schools—Fiction. 5. Christian life—Fiction.] I.
Curtis, Stacy, ill. II. Title.
  PZ7.S42675Mas 2008
  [Fic]—dc22
                                    2007049274

17 16 15 14 13 12   4 5 6 7 8 9 10 11 12

Contents

Book Fair

Flip, flop, flip, flop.

I waved a sealed white envelope in front of my friend Kayla. "Guess what I've got in here!"

Grinning, Kayla pulled a square yellow envelope out of her backpack. She waved hers in the air too. "Same thing I've got. Book fair money!"

Yay for school book fairs! They are like snack stands at baseball games. Only instead of picking candy or soda, you get to pick out a book or two. Plus, unlike candy or soda, you can have a book forever and enjoy it over and over again.

Well, I suppose you can also enjoy candy that's gum over and over again.

But that's not the point.

I bounced on my toes, waiting for Kayla to finish hanging up her coat. "I bet Mrs. Arnold scheduled our class to go to the book fair right after morning announcements."

"Really?" Kayla said.

"Sure," I nodded. "Otherwise she'd be jotting our daily assignments up on the board. Mrs. Arnold would never pass up a chance to give us work."

Kayla shrugged. "Maybe it's a trick."

"True. She might have some other super sneaky ideas up her sleeve," I said. "You never know with Mrs. Arnold. She is full of surprises."

I followed Kayla to her desk. "I want to buy a Purr-Purr Pretty Kitty book. And a fat, fuzzy marker. And an eraser that smells like strawberries. And a drawing book. And maybe even a funny animal poster."

"Me too," Kayla said. "I want to buy all those things too!"

From behind me, I heard my buddy Ryan groan. "You two are going to goop up the classroom with all that girl stuff."

Frowning, I turned around. "So? What are you getting? Basketball books?"

Ryan grinned. "No. I'm getting the new Super Cat comic book, a joke book, and *Juggling for Idiots*."

My jaw fell right open. Because those books sounded good too. Especially the idiotic one. And the joke book one. And the Super Cat one. With so many choices, how could I ever decide what to buy at the book fair?

As the possibilities raced through my head, the first bell rang. My other friend Lynette was already sitting at her seat. I waved as I sat down behind her. As usual, Lynette wore her black hair tied up in a huge, frilly hair bow.

I hate those frilly hair bow things. They get in my way of seeing the chalkboard.

I prefer wearing my long, straight, brown hair down.

Kayla wears her short, blond hair piggy-tailed. If she sat in front of me, at least I could see the chalkboard between the tails.

Anyway, Lynette also held an envelope. A pink one with purple butterflies on it.

She had drawn neat lines across the front —
probably with a ruler — and had made a list of
books she wanted. The letters looked as stiff
and straight as Mrs. Arnold's handwriting.

In first grade, I'm not sure neat
handwriting is normal. A lot of kids don't
even hold their pencils really right. Plus,
sometimes kids make letters backwards.

By the way, I asked Mrs. Arnold about
that once. "Mrs. Arnold," I said, "I don't
understand something. If I turn around
backwards, I'm still Meghan. If I stand on
my head, I'm still Meghan. If I spin around,
I'm Meghan, Meghan, Meghan, no matter
which way I face. So why is a letter *B* not
a letter *B* anymore when it's backwards or
upside down?"

Mrs. Arnold just said, "Because it's
something else."

I guess that kind of makes sense. Sometimes when I'm kangaroo bouncy or especially squirmy, my mom says I'm something else.

Anyway, like almost everything else about Lynette—her desk, backpack, clothes, lunch box—Lynette's handwriting looked neat.

Even so, Lynette is a friend, so I do not hold her neatness against her.

When announcements started, Lynette peeked over her shoulder at me. I smiled and gave her a thumbs-up. She smiled back and gave me a thumbs-up. I pointed to my envelope. She lifted hers up for me to see.

Leaning forward, I read the first item on her list. Lynette had drawn hearts around it, so I knew it had to be something extra special. Plus it had the words *super* and *secret* in it. So even though I didn't know what it was, I decided right then what I would buy with my book fair money.

I'd buy the first thing on Lynette's list.

A super secret something.

Super Secret Something

The book fair was set up near the school office. Hardcover books, paperbacks, computer games, pencils, pens, coloring books, friendship bracelets, puzzles, paper airplane kits, highlighters, bookmarks, posters, and all kinds of stuff crowded the area.

The hallway seemed like my suitcase when I pack for going to Grandma's—stuffed with junk and ready to burst.

I love those bookcases at the fair. They look like big, metal lunch boxes. Except the bookcases have wheels on the bottom. Plus they are filled with books instead of food. And they stand sideways.

At a small table, a parent volunteer sat with a cash box. Two other parents stood nearby to help kids pick out books and count their money.

Ryan made a beeline for the comic book section. Adam and Levi headed for the word puzzles and computer games. Mallory flipped through a Dr. Seuss book. Abigail hovered near the board books since her mom had told her to buy something for her baby brother.

Kayla zipped around like a crazed fly.

One minute I stood by myself trying to find Lynette, the next minute Kayla stood beside me tugging on my arm. Then she was gone and back again before I even found out what she wanted in the first place.

Kayla said, "Come on. Look what I found!"

I sighed. "What is it?"

But Kayla didn't answer. She grabbed my hand and dragged me along.

She also did a lot of pointing and squealing and grabbing and pointing and squealing and grabbing and pointing and squealing and grabbing and putting things back in the wrong spot.

Forget the fly. Kayla seemed more like a tornado.

A squealing, piggy-tailed tornado.

On the plus side, I did get to see almost every book and toy and office supply at the fair in less than five minutes.

Finally Kayla spotted Lynette and dashed over to her, lugging me along.

Lynette already cradled three books in her arms. Her eyes seemed to sparkle when she saw us.

Kayla blurted out, "What did you get?"

Lynette said, "Remember the Nursery Rhyme Number Mystery series?"

Kayla and I nodded. Mrs. Arnold had read two of those mysteries to us at the beginning of the school year. They were called *One Potato Perpetrator* and *Treacherous Two for the Show.*

I understood the books better after watching the news on television one night. That's when I figured out that a perpetrator is a sneaky bad guy, and treacherous is how weathermen describe slippery ice in a state called Colorado.

I believe they make pet collars in Collar-rado. Collars come in handy when people walk their tiny poodles on treacherous ice. They can hold on to their collars and keep their pets from slipping away.

But there were no poodles or perpetrators here — just Lynette holding up a paperback. The cover had three dark shadows and creepy writing on it. "This is book number three in the series: *Three Robbing-You-Blind Mice*."

I held up a finger. "Let me guess. The farmer's wife did it. With a carving knife."

Lynette rolled her eyes at me. Then we both laughed.

But Kayla's eyes went wide. "Really?" she gasped. "How did you know?"

Apparently Kayla didn't pay much attention during preschool.

"Never mind," Lynette said, shaking her head. "I also got a Purr-Purr Pretty Kitty book."

I said, "I wanted one of those too. Where are they?"

Lynette pointed. Before I could move, Kayla zipped over, snatched two off the shelf, and raced back. She skidded to a stop like a snowball going *splat* against the wall. Panting, she handed one to me. She tucked the other one under her arm. "What else?"

Then Lynette held up a fat book with a purple velvet cover. It had the words *super* and *secret* on the front. And it had a golden lock and key.

"I bought a diary," she said.

My heart went *bump-bump, bump-bump*. "Can I see it?"

Lynette placed it into my hands. The

purple cover felt soft and fuzzy, like a baby chick. I rubbed my fingers over it before unfastening the lock. I opened the book. I flipped through a few pages. Then a few more. Then a few more. Then more, more, more.

My body sagged. I frowned. "This book is broken."

"What?" Lynette said.

"It's broken," I repeated. "The pages are all blank."

Lynette laughed. "That's because it's a diary."

I wrinkled my nose. "What's a diary?"

"It's a book that you write in," Lynette said.

I said, "Exactly what do you write?"

Lynette shrugged. "You write about things you do each day that you want to remember. Or you could write a poem. Or a story. Or draw a picture. The lock on it means no one else can read it unless you show them. It keeps everything you write or draw secret."

Kayla and I both squealed and clapped. Because, let me tell you, nothing is more fun than a secret!

"Where are they?" I asked.

Lynette pointed. Just like before, Kayla zipped, snatched, and raced back.

When our class finally returned from the book fair, all three of us had a super secret diary with a purple velvet cover and a golden lock and key.

Now I just needed a secret.

Paige

I believe the school looks and feels different on rainy days. For one thing, when rain pours down the classroom windows instead of sun pouring in, everything seems dark and shadowy.

If you don't understand what dark and shadowy feels like, turn off the lights in your room sometime and sit quietly for a few minutes. You'll get it.

Also, when it rains, there are usually a

few wet umbrellas lying around. That makes the air smell damp.

If you don't understand what damp smells like, the next time your mom does the laundry, open the dryer door, pull out a wet towel, and take a big sniff. It will smell damp.

Just remember to put the towel back and turn the dryer on again when you are finished. Otherwise, your mom might get kind of annoyed and make you fold all the laundry yourself.

At least, that's what my mom did.

Besides making everything dark and shadowy and dampish-smelling, the rain gurgling and splattering outside like a gigantic leaky faucet always makes our inside voices sound hushed and muffled.

And if you don't understand what hushed

and muffled sounds like, try plugging your ears and talking in a whisper. That's how it sounds in a classroom on a rainy day.

By lunchtime on the day of the book fair, rain was pounding on the ground outside.

So that meant the school felt dark, shadowy, damp, hushed, and muffled.

Rain also meant inside recess after we ate lunch.

In the cafeteria, Lynette, Kayla, and I decided inside recess would be the perfect time to start writing in our diaries.

When the recess teacher brought us back to the classroom, we claimed the reading couch. We snuggled down together side by side. On our laps lay our diaries. In one hand, we each held a fuzzy writing pen. In the other hand, we each held a golden key.

At the same moment, we opened our

golden locks. The diary pages folded down like flower petals. Clean. White. Fresh. New.

Just waiting to hold our secrets.

Except I didn't have any secrets. I blankly looked at those blank pages thinking blankly about nothing but blankness. Finally I grumped, "How do we start?"

Lynette glanced at me. "You start like it's a letter to a friend. You say Dear Diary, and then write what you're thinking."

"Do we have to say Dear Diary?" I said. "Because I don't like the name Diary. It sounds too much like stinky diarrhea. Plus, what happens if I mix the letters up like I sometimes do in handwriting? Then diary becomes something else. Something like the word *dairy*. Dear *Dairy*. Like a moo-moo dairy cow. Or *dreary*. I sure don't want

19

to goof and write Dear *Dreary*."

Lynette was frowning.

"Who came up with the name Diary anyway?" I asked. "It doesn't make sense. Why not just call it Blank Book? Maybe we could call ours Violet, since the cover is purple. I like writing Dear Violet much better."

By this time Lynette was squeezing her pen so hard her knuckles were white. "It's called a diary. I don't know why. I don't care why. You're just supposed to start with Dear Diary and that's all," she said through clenched teeth.

I ignored her. "I know! I'll call it Page. P-a-g-e! Because it's full of pages."

Lynette lowered her voice so it almost growled. "You mean P-a-*i*-g-e. That's how you spell the name Paige. P-a-g-e just means a piece of paper. But you can't call it Paige anyway because it's not just a page. It's a diary!"

This time I frowned at Lynette. "It's my diary. I can call it whatever I want."

Lynette said, "No. You have to call it Diary."

I shot back, "Do not!"

"Do too!"

"I like Paige better."

"You can't call it Paige," Lynette said with a loud voice.

I said even louder, "You don't know everything!"

Lynette said even louder, "I know you can't call it Paige!"

"Oh, yeah?" I shouted. "Watch me."

In big, fat letters, I wrote DEAR PAIGE and shoved it under her nose.

Lynette's cheeks turned red. Her eyes bulged. She jumped to her feet and stomped away from me. "It's Dear Diary, Diary, *DIARY*!" she yelled.

"Dear Paige, Paige, *PAIGE*!" I yelled back.

The recess teacher ran into the room just then. I tried to explain about Lynette's stubbornness, but Lynette kept interrupting me. We both ended up spending the rest of recess sitting at our desks.

Slumping in my chair behind Lynette, I

glared at her frilly hair bow. It wasn't fair. I didn't do anything wrong. Why should I be punished? My stomach tightened as I tried to hold all my secret, angry thoughts inside.

Then I remembered Paige. My diary named Paige could hold my secret, angry thoughts for me.

I picked up a pencil. I scratched down words about how mean Lynette treated me, how much she brags, and how this whole thing was all her fault.

As I wrote, the classroom sure didn't seem hushed and muffled anymore. Not for the rest of recess, and not the whole rest of the day.

But it still felt dark, shadowy, and damp.

More Secrets

With a gentle tap on my shoulder, Mom woke me. "Good morning, sunshine."

Groaning, I rolled over and pulled my blankets over my head.

Mom said, "Time to get up, Meghan. Open your eyes."

I squeezed my eyes shut.

"Come on. It's Tuesday," Mom said. "School day."

And then she flipped on the lights.

Let me tell you, when that bright light comes on, it hits your face like a bowl of cold spaghetti. And, *blammo*, you wake up. When Thomas Edison invented the lightbulb, I believe he meant it to be used for the good of all mankind. I bet he had no idea parents would use it as a weapon against sleepy children.

So that's how my day started. With *blammo* bright lights in my eyes and not enough sleep.

I blamed Lynette. If she hadn't been such a know-it-all about diaries yesterday, I wouldn't have written those secret, angry words about her.

It was the secret, angry words that kept me up all night because I kept thinking about them and getting more and more upset with Lynette. That led to bad dreams.

Which led to not enough sleep. Which led to *blammo* bright lights in my eyes.

Obviously Thomas Edison didn't know people like Lynette who could rob my sleep. Or people like my mom who could misuse his invention.

At least the rain had stopped overnight.

Plus, on the bus ride to school, Ryan told me some jokes from his new joke book. I liked the month jokes. What's an ant's favorite month? March! A falling snowflake's favorite month? Descend-brrrrrrrr. A spider's favorite month? Web-ruary. A nurse's favorite month? Doctor-ber. A monkey's favorite month? Ape-ril.

When Ryan ran out of jokes, I asked, "What about your *Juggling for Idiots* book? Have you learned how to juggle yet?"

Shrugging, Ryan said. "Not yet. The

problem is, I'm not an idiot. So I don't always understand the directions because they are written for idiots."

Without thinking, I blurted, "Then you should ask Lynette to read them for you."

Ryan frowned. "That was a pretty stinky thing to say. Lynette's not an idiot."

My face felt hot, and I knew I was blushing. I turned my head away so Ryan wouldn't see. Somehow that just made me madder at Lynette. "Yeah," I said, "But she's a big, braggy know-it-all."

Ryan said, "No, she's not. She's nice! I like her."

"Oh, really?" I huffed. "Who do you like better, Lynette or me?"

Ryan squinted at me. "I like you both. It's not a contest."

"I knew it! You like her better!"

Ryan stammered, "I didn't say that!"

"Humph," I said, folding my arms. Ignoring him, I glared out the window the rest of the way to school.

I pushed ahead of Ryan when the bus unloaded. As soon as I finished hanging up my coat, I yanked my diary named Paige out of my backpack and sat down at my desk. Before morning announcements started, I wrote new sentences about Ryan and more about Lynette. I used big, dark letters like stabs of lightning across the white paper.

Kayla interrupted me. "Are you writing in your dear diary?"

"Paige," I muttered. "I'm writing in Paige."

Kayla peeked over my shoulder. "Are you writing about the book fair?"

I quick hid Paige with my arm. "No."

"I know," Kayla said. "You're writing about noodles!"

"No," I said. "Go away."

"How about poodles?"

"No."

"Puddles!"

"NO!"

"BEETLES! BOTTLES! BATTLES!"

"NO! NO! NO!"

"SNORKELS!"

"NOooo!"

Kayla took a big breath. "I've got it!" she cried. "DUCKS!"

I snapped Paige closed. I jumped to my feet. I leaned toward Kayla. "NO. I'm not writing about ducks. I'm writing about none-of-your-business. What's wrong with you this morning anyway? Did you swallow a Dr. Seuss book or something?"

Kayla looked quite pleased with herself. "I read *Fox in Socks* all by myself. Eight times. Aren't you proud of me?"

I glared at her. "There aren't any snorkels in that story. Or ducks wearing snorkels."

Kayla grinned. "I know. But I like the words *snorkel* and *duck*. They are fun to say. In fact, I like them so much that I'm going to write them in my dear diary."

Humming, Kayla pranced to her desk. She spent the last two minutes before morning announcements doodling in her diary. And chanting, "Snorkel, snorkel, duck, duck, snorkel, duck, snorkel."

I spent the last two minutes writing even more secret, angry words in Paige. About snorkels and ducks.

And Kayla.

Later, I ate lunch with Kayla and Lynette.

We laughed and jumped rope together at recess. They did not even suspect that I had written some not-so-nice things about them in Paige.

It was my secret.

That night when I said my prayers, part of me wanted to hide under my covers the same way I hid Paige from Kayla.

The other part turned on the light and reread Paige so I could remember all the things my friends did that bugged me.

And this time, I held it against them.

Reading Buddies

On Wednesday afternoons, Mrs. Robison's fourth-grade class visits us. I like fourth graders because they are still kids but thcy act almost grown-up. That means they still like cereal box prizes and watching cartoons. But they can wake themselves up in the morning. And I believe they can even change their own lightbulbs.

I bet if Thomas Edison knew that, he'd glow with pride.

By the way, do you know how many fourth graders it takes to change a lightbulb? I don't. But Ryan says it takes just one, if he's really bright.

Anyway, the first graders in Mrs. Arnold's class pair up with fourth-grade reading buddies. Like a nice batch of chocolate chip cookies, there are just enough reading buddies for each first grader to have one apiece.

Let me tell you, whoever invented reading buddies was a real brain-o. Because, next to chocolate chip cookies and lightbulbs, reading buddies are one of the best things ever invented.

Reading buddies do more than just visit once a week to read with you. Sometimes they listen to you read. Plus they help you figure out hard words.

Best of all, if your reading buddy sees you in the hallway or on the playground or hiding under the piano in the music room, he smiles and waves at you. It always makes me feel warm and fuzzy and kangaroo bouncy when a big kid smiles and waves at me.

My reading buddy is named Michael Rimsky.

I like Michael Rimsky. He is thinnish and medium-tallish. When he reads, the pages reflect off his round glasses. Michael changes his voice for different characters in stories. His voice goes high and squeaky for a girl, low and growly for a bad guy, and regular for a regular guy.

The thing I like best of all about Michael is his hair, which is red and sticky-uppy, like he just rolled out of bed and didn't bother to comb it.

This Wednesday Michael brought along a joke book to read. Michael read several pages. The jokes started sounding a little familiar when he said, "What has four legs, eats grass, says moo, and drinks cement?"

Real slow, I said, "A cow?"

"That's right!" Michael grinned. "A cow. I just threw in the cement to make it hard. Get it? The cement makes it hard? Here's another one. How is a small bucket like a sick man?"

I shrugged, still thinking about the cow joke.

"They are both a little pail!" Michael said. "Get it? Pale? Pail?"

I groaned. "I've heard that before."

When Michael started on month jokes, I stopped him. "I know all these jokes. Let me see the cover."

After Michael showed me, I said, "That's the same joke book my friend Ryan picked out at the book fair."

Michael slouched. "It's no fun telling jokes when the other person knows all the answers. We'll have to read something else. Did you get anything at the book fair?"

"Yes," I said. I listed my books one by one. Michael made a face each time until I said the word *diary*.

Then Michael sat up real straight. "A diary?"

"Paige," I said. "I call my diary Paige."

"Let's read Paige. That sounds better than all those other books."

My heart went *bump-bump*. "Really?"

"C'mon," Michael said. "It's not like you've got some big, dark secret you're trying to hide. Is it?"

"No," I snapped.

Michael paused. "Well?"

My heart sped up. *BUMP-bump, BUMP-bump*. Sticky sweat formed on my hands. I rubbed them on my pants.

"Please?" Michael said.

Licking my lips, I glanced around the room. I saw Kayla snuggled up on the reading couch with her reading buddy, a girl named Jenna. Lynette and her reading buddy, Lissie, bent over a book in the corner of the room by Mrs. Arnold's desk. Ryan and Robbie slouched up near the windows. All sat out of earshot.

Good, I thought. For some reason, I didn't want my friends to hear what I had written.

My stomach fluttered. After all, I didn't write things I expected someone else to see.

What would Michael think? Would he still smile and wave at me after he heard about my rotten friends? Maybe he'd feel sorry for me.

Michael cleared his throat. "I'm waiting."

I gulped.

Sticks and Stones

I made up my mind. Taking another quick glance around the room, I snuck to my desk, snatched out Paige, and brought it to Michael.

Michael rubbed his fingers over the velvet cover. "So this is Paige. Very fuzzy. And locked."

I fished around in my pocket. "Sorry. I'll find the key."

Shaking his head, Michael handed it

back. "These are your secret words. You get to do the honors."

"Honors?" I said, pulling out the tiny golden key.

Michael said. "That means you get to read to me."

Putting his arms behind his head, he leaned back and smiled.

I shrugged. And opened Paige. And took a big breath. "Dear Paige . . ."

I started off OK. But as I read, my voice got softer and softer. Reading my words out loud . . . well, they didn't sound bold or right, like I thought they would. They just sounded small and mean.

When Michael's smile fell off his face, I started whispering. When he frowned, my words came out in a croak. When Michael shook his head, I stopped.

Michael studied me with his big brown eyes. I don't know why, but I couldn't look back at him. Instead, I ducked my head and stared at my shoes. I felt like I had just failed a math test or something.

But then I got mad!

Lynette bragged. Kayla bugged. And Ryan betrayed me by taking Lynette's side, which wasn't fair at all.

I only wrote the truth.

My hands curled into fists. I lifted my chin. I stared at Michael with eyes hard like marbles, waiting for him to comment.

Michael sat in silence for about a billion seconds, like he was thinking hard. Finally he sighed. "You used some strong words."

I nodded.

Michael continued. "You could do a lot of damage with big, powerful words like that. You could crush someone," he snapped his fingers, "just like that."

"Not-uh," I snorted. "Everyone I know says that sticks and stones may break my bones, but words will never harm me."

Michael gave me a sad look. "They say that, but it's not true."

"Sure it is. I just read them. No one has any bruises, do they?"

"Some bruises can't be seen," Michael said. He tapped his chest. "I got hurt like that once. Inside. Hurts every time I think about some of the words a so-called friend used against me."

"Who was it?" I asked.

Michael lowered his voice. "He's over by the backpacks."

I looked. A large boy hunched next to Levi. With his size and rounded belly, he

44

reminded me of a gigantic beanbag chair.

"His name's Steven. He moved here before the school year started. Since he didn't know anyone, I invited him over to play. Introduced him to kids in the neighborhood."

"That was nice," I said.

"His mom appreciated it," Michael said. "Told me I was an answer to prayer. I liked that—helping someone."

He whispered, and I leaned forward to hear better. "When school started, I guess he didn't think I was popular enough. Sometimes when I sat by him at lunch, he moved away to another table. Made a big showy fuss about it too. It embarrassed me so much I just avoided him. Then he started calling me names on the playground. I never understood why he did that. Maybe because it made the other kids laugh. My mom said that maybe he thought making fun of me would somehow make him look better."

Peeking Steven's direction, Michael murmured, "Believe me, Meghan Rose, those words hurt. And they still hurt me, like poking a blister filled with pus. Sometimes I remember what he said, and I feel like a bag of garbage."

Tears stung my eyes. "Oh, no, Michael! You're not a bag of garbage!"

"I know." Michael ran his fingers through his messy hair. "Listen, do you like Lynette and Kayla and Ryan?"

"Yes," I said.

"Don't ever let them see that diary then. How would they feel?"

"They'll never read it," I said, locking it up. "It's secret."

"Yeah?" Michael said. "Secrets are something you hold close to your heart. Why would you keep angry words close to your heart? Besides, secrets have a way of slipping out. And rumors have a way of spreading."

I swallowed. Hard. And pulled Paige to my chest. Just then, Mrs. Arnold gave a two-minute warning. An excited buzz of talk shot through the room while reading buddies collected their books. Kids quickly quieted when Mrs. Arnold raised her finger and counted to three.

As the thought *Oh, no, what have I done?* swarmed into my mind, Michael nudged me. "I like you, Meghan."

His words chased that panicky thought away like a warm hug chases away your fears. It felt so good to hear him say that.

"You're funny and sweet and kind."

The words melted around me like butter on toast. A smile crept to my lips and grew bigger and bigger.

"You're smart and bouncy and interesting."

Mrs. Robison signaled.

Grinning like a fox, Michael stood. "Wonder why you're smiling so big and beautiful, Meghan Rose. Was it something I said?"

I laughed and nodded.

"Yes!" Michael said with a superhero-sounding voice. He flexed his arm muscles. "Word power!"

I watched as Michael lined up. Sneering, Steven elbowed in front of him. Michael winced and rubbed his chest. Then Steven said something, and a few kids behind

Michael laughed. Michael's face went red. His body seemed to deflate like a flat tire. Still, he gave me a weak smile before waving good-bye.

With a lump in my throat, I waved back. *Looks like that Steven has some word power too*, I thought.

Word Power

Michael's praise sang through my heart all day. I'm sweet! I'm smart! I'm funny! But the memory of how Steven had so easily crushed Michael with just a few words in line bothered me.

By bedtime Wednesday night my stomach was twisted in knots. I needed to know more about word power.

I puffed my pillows so I could sit up comfortably and waited for Dad to come tuck me in. Finally he opened my bedroom door. "Ready for a story?"

I shook my head. "Not tonight. I want to ask you some questions instead."

Sitting down on the edge of my bed, Dad asked, "What's up?"

"What do you know about words?"

Dad gave a sneaky grin. "Well, words can be little like *boo* and *you*." He poked me in the ribs when he said each word to make me giggle.

"And they can be big like . . ." he wriggled his fingers, ready to give a big tickle, tickle, tickle.

". . . like . . ." he said, tickle fingers waving. I tensed up to resist.

". . . like . . ." My shoulders scrunched. His tickle fingers shot down on my stomach. ". . . SUPERSONIC CELEBRATION!"

"HAHAHAHAHA!" I said, kicking my blankets.

Chuckling, Dad leaned back. "Anything else you want to know?"

I gulped some air to settle down. "Do words have power?"

"Sure," Dad said. "After all, God used words to create the world."

My mouth made an O shape. "That's right. I remember. He said stuff like, 'Let there be light.' And *blammo*! Lights came on even before Thomas Edison invented the lightbulb."

Dad nodded. "Did you know it took Thomas Edison over three thousand tries to make the lightbulb work?"

"Wowie," I said. "And all God had to do was just whisper the word *stars*, and all the stars twinkled to life."

We sat in silence for a bit as I bounced that idea around in my mind. Of course, it made sense, that God's words would have power like that. But . . .

"Do regular old words have power too?" I asked.

Dad raised an eyebrow. "What do you mean? Words make laws, coaches motivate teams with words, people express opinions with words—"

"Not those words!" I said. "My words. What can my words do?"

"Hmm," Dad said. "Do you remember last summer when we took Kayla to the pool and she was afraid to jump off the diving board?"

I nodded. "I yelled at her not to be afraid. She could do it. She just had to fall in."

"She fell, all right," Dad said. "Made a

big belly-flopping splash when she smacked the water."

"And then she was so excited, she got out and jumped again!"

"Can you think of any other time your words had power?" Dad asked.

"When Ryan messed up his talent show tryout, he nearly died of embarrassment. I told him he was brave and that dribbling two basketballs was amazing. He didn't feel so bad after that," I said, and thought for a second.

"Also, when Lynette got stage fright, I talked to her in the bathroom. I made her stop crying and offered to help her."

My voice trailed off as I thought about that time.

"So, what do *you* know about words?" Dad finally asked.

I took a big breath. "My words can help people get over being a scaredy-cat. My words can cheer people up. Best of all, my words can give people hope and help them believe in themselves."

"Interesting," Dad said. "I guess what the Bible says is true. The right words said at the right time are like apples of gold."

Apples of gold. They sounded priceless. Inspiring. Lovely. Sweet.

And what filled the pages of my diary named Paige?

Wormy, rotten, apples-of-mold words.

Like Steven's words.

"My words can do the opposite too, can't they?" I asked.

"Words can tear down and destroy like fire," Dad agreed. "The Bible also says a harsh word can stir up anger."

I bit my lip. "Thanks, Dad. I think I'll pray by myself tonight."

Dad kissed my forehead. "You sure?"

"Yes," I said. "I'm sure."

And I was sure. I needed to talk to God. I needed to use some powerful words. And the most powerful words I needed to use were *I'm sorry*.

Chatter Really Matters

Dad forgot to pull down my window shade Wednesday night, so the sun woke me up the next day.

By the way, I believe there is a huge difference between electric lights and sunlight in the morning.

I mean, when Mom flips a switch, *blammo*, light hits my eyes. The sun puts light in my eyes too. And both shine bright enough to wake me up. But the thing is, like

I said before, bedroom lights shock you like a bowl of cold spaghetti in your face. The sun feels more like a gentle hand warming your cheek.

Maybe Thomas Edison should have factored that sunlight information into his lightbulb invention.

Anyway, I hopped right out of bed. I had a lot of laughing and playing and having fun to do today. That's my job as a kid. To laugh, play, and have fun.

Oh, and to learn. Especially in Mrs. Arnold's class.

Just thinking about the day made me twirl around my room.

Maybe on the bus Ryan would bring the Super Cat book he got from the book fair. We could read it together. I could also find out if he knew how to juggle yet.

I couldn't wait for a rowdy round of jump roping at recess with Lynette and Kayla, my best friends in the whole wide world.

Maybe I'd spy my reading buddy, Michael, in the hallway today.

Plus, a carton of chocolate milk waited for me at lunch.

Smiling, I pulled on my socks. Today would be a great day.

And it was great . . . until the end of the school day.

That's when Mrs. Arnold did something she hardly ever does. She finished teaching her social study lesson early.

I always thought some crazy law prevented things like that from happening.

Mrs. Arnold glanced at her watch. "We have fifteen minutes before we have to get ready for home. Let's have an extra Chatter

Matters. If you like, you may bring a book along this time."

Everyone cheered, even me. That's because I didn't know that this Chatter Matters time would not be a great thing.

Chatter Matters means sitting in groups of two or three and whisper-talking together without arguing, tattling, or bragging. We can sit all over the room too, even under Mrs. Arnold's desk.

As usual, Lynette, Kayla, and I all scrambled to the reading couch.

Giggling, we leaned back on the cushions. We heard Ryan's voice behind us. Without a peep, the three of us peeked over the top of the couch to spy on him.

Ryan sat between Adam and Levi. Since I knew from the morning bus ride that Ryan could now juggle two balls, I guessed that he held the juggling book on his lap. Especially since he kept pointing and waving his arms around.

Lynette said, "I forgot! Mrs. Arnold said we could bring a book."

Kayla whisper-squealed. "I know! Let's read our diaries."

Before you could say Thomas Edison, Lynette and Kayla raced back to their desks, grabbed their diaries, and flew back.

I stumbled along behind them. My knees wobbled. My stomach gurgled.

When I prayed last night, God and I talked about word power. I woke up wanting to use words to grow a few smiles the way Michael grew mine.

You know what, though? I don't quite recall the problem of revealing to my friends the secret, angry words hidden in my diary coming up in my conversation with God. I'm pretty sure I would have remembered that part.

As I fumbled at my desk, all I could think about was how my dark, ugly, apples-of-mold words would steal all the happy away from Kayla and Lynette if I read them out loud.

With shaky hands, I stuffed Paige under my shirt. My heart throbbed as I shuffled back to the couch. I slouched deep down in the cushions feeling like a cartoon character trying to snuff out a stick of dynamite about to go *ka-boom*.

Kayla said, "I'll go first. I didn't write a lot, but I did draw pictures. This is me. See my piggy-tails? Here's Lynette."

Lynette leaned closer to Kayla. She laughed, then pointed. "What's that big scribble on top of my head? It takes up half the page."

"That's your hair bow," Kayla said. "And this is Meghan. I made the lines for your hair extra kangaroo-bouncy. That's why all the squiggles are everywhere. Then I drew a bunch of snorkels and ducks . . ."

Kayla turned several pages, probably all filled with snorkels and ducks. Then she stopped. "I drew a picture of all three of us together. Look!"

I didn't want to look, but Kayla shoved her diary under my face. Kayla had drawn three smiley-faced stick people holding hands. She put big, pink hearts all around them. In even bigger purple letters, she had printed the words *bass fins*.

Bass fish do have fins, but writing about that didn't make sense with the picture. Pink

hearts. No water. It all seemed a little fishy. Still, Kayla had made some of the letters backwards, maybe she meant something else.

Kayla said, "This page says *best friends*."

When she said those words, a smile exploded across my face like a firecracker in July.

Then I remembered what I wrote about Kayla, and that smile fell right off my face.

Kayla snapped her diary shut. "That's all. Who's next?"

Lynette and Kayla looked at me.

I slouched further into the couch.

And prayed in my head that Mrs. Arnold would get back to her normal self, call off Chatter Matters, and give us a surprise test or something instead.

Apples of Gold

Lynette sighed, fiddling with the lock on her diary. "I guess I'll go next. But I didn't make any pictures. And you have to remember, people don't usually share what they write in their diaries."

Suspicion crept into my mind. Why did Lynette sigh? Why did she remind us about people not sharing their diaries?

Here I was worried about hurting her feelings, and all along I bet she had written some mean things about me in her diary. In very neat letters.

Something that could do more damage than sticks and stones.

My back went stiff. I narrowed my eyes. "Are you afraid of sharing your secrets?"

Lynette blinked at me. "No," she said, a little too quickly, if you ask me.

Kayla started bouncing up and down. "Well, hurry up then!"

Lynette bit her lip. "Maybe Meghan should go first."

I gritted my teeth. I scowled my eyebrows together. *Lynette must be hiding something!* I thought.

Kayla kept bouncing. "OK, Meghan, your turn."

"Fine," I snapped.

Glaring at Lynette, I whipped my diary

named Paige out from under my shirt. I grabbed my golden key and fitted it into the lock.

Just then, Kayla did a big, floppy bounce that sent her diary flying. She never locked it, so when it hit the floor, it fell open at my feet with a *smack*.

Open to the "bass fins" page.

I stopped. *Best friends*. Lynette and Kayla were my best friends. My best friends in the whole wide world. Why would I ever, ever, ever, *ever* want to hurt them?

Like snapping off a lightbulb with the flip of a switch, my anger shut off. Maybe Lynette did write something mean. Maybe not. But I was done with mean words. I only wanted apples of gold.

Taking a big, calming breath, I picked up Kayla's diary and handed it back.

Kayla kept bouncing. "Thanks!"

I turned to Lynette. "Why don't you want to go next?"

Lynette's face turned red. "It's just that . . . well, Kayla's diary was so fun . . ."

Kayla kept bouncing. "Yay for me! I'm fun!"

". . . and so colorful and bright . . ."

Kayla kept bouncing. "Yay for me! I'm colorful and bright!"

Lynette continued. "And my diary isn't like that. I just wrote about what I did each day. You know, getting dressed, eating lunch, doing homework. So I was afraid that . . . maybe you would think I was boring."

That's why she didn't want to go next? I laughed inside my head and smiled on the outside.

"You will not bore us any more than

usual," I said, patting Lynette's knee. "Besides, after Kayla, we could use a break from excitement."

Kayla kept bouncing. "Yay for me! I'm exciting!" Then she looped an arm around both of us. "Let's all act fun and colorful and bright and exciting!"

That's when Kayla got us all bouncing and laughing on the reading couch.

Which, of course, got us all in trouble.

So we had to spend the rest of our Chatter Matters time sitting at our desks with our heads down.

As I sat, the words *best friends* kept swirling around through my mind.

And, let me tell you, if anything shimmered like apples of gold, it was those words.

Meghan Rose Has a Secret

By the time Mom flicked on the lights Friday morning, I had figured some things out about words.

Nice words have power. I know because I've felt it.

When Mom tells me she loves me, the words fall around my heart like a snuggly, warm blanket.

When Dad tells me I'm strong, I believe I could fly over a mountain. Or scramble up a steep hill. Or at least maybe climb out of bed.

Not-so-nice words have power too. I know, because I've felt that. When Mrs. Arnold tells me to sit at my desk and put my head down, my stomach and my thoughts churn. When someone grumps at me, my whole body sags.

Words on paper have power too. For example, Mrs. Arnold has this poster in her room that says, "Success happens when you refuse to give up."

I asked her once what that meant.

She said, "If you want the seeds of your dreams to grow, you must water them with a little bit of sweat."

I remember scrunching up my face at her. "Why not use a watering can on your pillow?"

Mrs. Arnold had sighed. "It means you have to work hard and keep trying if you want to get what you want."

So now whenever I read that poster, I always work harder.

Plus also when I read the Bible, those words have a lot of power. One night I couldn't sleep because of the big, dark shadows in my room. Mom read me a verse from the Bible that said God's unfailing love surrounds me.

Unfailing means you can count on it no matter what. Sort of like Mrs. Arnold giving a spelling test every Friday. Except not exactly since sometimes we don't have school on Friday because of a holiday.

Anyway, after Mom read about God's unfailing love, the shadows didn't seem so big anymore. I fell asleep super quick.

Anyway, that's how Friday started. Again with *blammo* bright lights in my eyes. But also with a little bit of light in my heart.

When I got to school, I saw my reading buddy, Michael, in the hall. When he waved at me, an idea popped *BLAM* into my head.

Michael was right about secrets. You hold them close to your heart. I don't want to keep angry words in my diary named Paige. Keeping them in Paige also kept them in my mind, like the double-fudge brownie Mom had tucked in my lunch box today. Even though I couldn't see it right now, I kept thinking about it and how good it would taste.

I didn't want to keep thinking about those mean, old words. They tasted rotten anyway.

Not at all like double-fudge brownies. Or apples of gold.

After I hung up my backpack and coat, I snuck Paige under my shirt. Then I asked Mrs. Arnold if I could go to the bathroom.

Since it was Friday, Mrs. Arnold waved me out without asking any questions.

In the bathroom, I locked myself in a stall, sat down, and balanced Paige on my lap. Ignoring the faint laughter of kids in the hall echoing off the bathroom walls and the smell of pine cleaner, I opened the lock and tucked the key back in my pocket.

"Paige, I hate to do this to you," I said. "But as long as I keep those secret, angry words, I'll keep the mad feelings too."

One by one, I ripped every page I had written on out of my diary. Just like someone might rip a bandage off a cut. OUCH!

I tore each page into tiny pieces.

Finally, I stuffed all my trash into the wastebasket.

Paige still had a purple velvet cover and a golden lock and key. But once again, Paige's pages looked clean. White. Fresh. New.

Just the way I felt inside.

Now I just needed a secret.

I skipped all the way back to the classroom. Setting Paige down on the top of my desk, I glanced at the clock. Five more minutes until morning announcements. I had time.

I snuck up behind Mrs. Arnold and locked her in a fierce bear hug. "I love you, Mrs. Arnold."

I expected her to say, "That's nice. Find a seat."

Instead, a smile tugged at the corner of her mouth and she hugged me back.

After that, I zoomed across the room and hugged Kayla. She squealed and hugged me back. Plus we jumped up and down a few times. I didn't say anything because Kayla hugged me so hard I couldn't breathe.

When she let go, I spotted Ryan and hugged him.

More like tackled him into the reading couch, really, since I had a running start and launched myself at him.

Ryan gave me a goofy grin when I said, "You're funny. I like you."

But then Adam glanced our way, and Ryan made a strangling sound. "Augh! Cooties!" he said, and tried to push me away. I only let go when we fell onto the floor. No need to overdo it.

Lynette helped me untangle myself from Ryan. After I staggered to my feet, I hugged her too.

"You're very . . . neat," I said.

Since I'm taller than Lynette, I believe her head got squished up under my arm.

Her voice sounded muffled when she said, "Thanks!"

I let go. "Ready for Chatter Matters today?"

Lynette smoothed her shirt down. "Yes.

If Mrs. Arnold lets us bring a book again, we can both read our diaries."

I shook my head. "Sorry. I'm starting my diary over, so it's blank right now. But I've got some powerful words and new secrets to write in it. Loads and loads of them."

When Lynette narrowed her eyes at me, I winked. "Secrets I plan on sharing every day. With or without Chatter Matters time."

Chatter Matters

1. What books would you like to buy at a book fair? Why?

2. The wisest man in the Old Testament, King Solomon, had some wisdom about words that he wrote down. Read what he said in Proverbs 12:25, 15:1, 16:24, and 18:4. Can you explain one of these verses in your own words?

3. Did you know God has a secret? Want to find out what it is? Look up Colossians 1:27. If you think you understand the secret, whisper it in someone's ear. If you don't understand God's secret, ask a parent to help you out.

4. Tell about a time when you felt discouraged and someone said something that cheered you up. Have you ever cheered someone up? What did you say or do?

5. Just like Meghan Rose, sometimes we get mad at our friends. Meghan talked with God about some of her feelings. What helps you feel better when you are angry?

Blam! – Great Activity Ideas

1. **Make your own diary.** You need a notebook (not spiral bound), fabric (longer than the notebook on all sides), tacky glue (or hot glue used with adult supervision), and scissors. Open up the notebook and lay it down flat on the fabric. Trim around the notebook, leaving about ½ inch of extra material all the way around. These edges will be flaps to fold in later. (You could first draw a guideline on the fabric around the notebook with a pencil so you can see where to cut.)

Spread the fabric out again. Make sure the side you want to be on the cover is facing down. Apply glue to the front and back covers of the notebook. Then lay the notebook back down, centered on the fabric, and press the sticky sides firmly onto the fabric. Be careful to keep the edges free. Next, fold in and glue down the ½-inch edges of fabric like wrapping a present. Glue down the first and last notebook pages (or pieces of card stock cut to fit) over the inside fabric edges to cover them up. Allow glue to dry. If you like, decorate the cover with fabric paint, buttons, or permanent markers.

2. Make a pencil topper. You need hot glue (used with adult supervision), one chenille wire, paper (or cardboard or foam), and markers. First, color a small picture (a little larger than a quarter) on the paper. Cut this out. Cut the chenille wire in half. Twist one half around the pencil, then gently pull it off. The wire should be curled into a spiral. Hot glue the small picture to one end of the curled chenille wire. Hot glue the other end of the chenille wire to the metal ring that holds the eraser on the pencil.

3. Write kind notes to friends. Give the notes at school or send them in the mail. You could write about things you like about your friends or thank them for the ways they are friends to you. If you want, you could find some Bible verses that have encouraging messages and include those in your notes. Ask a parent to help you spell out what you want to say.

4. Be a reading buddy. Pick out a book that you liked when you were younger. Snuggle up and read to a younger friend you know, maybe a family member or a neighbor. You can also read to your parents or a pet.

5. Eat an apple of gold. In the grocery store, you can find apples called Golden Delicious apples. Remember, powerful words are like apples of gold—sweet to the soul and healthy for the body. They can cheer up others and give hope!

To all of Meghan's teachers,
especially Mrs. Arnold—LZS

For Sally—SC

Lori Z. Scott graduated from Wheaton College
eons ago. She is a second-grade teacher, a wife, the
mother of two busy teenagers, and a writer. Lori has
published over one hundred articles, short stories,
devotions, puzzles, and poems and has contributed
to over a dozen books.

In her spare time Lori loves doodling, reading the
Sunday comics, and making up lame jokes.

You can find out more about Lori and her books
at www.MeghanRoseSeries.com.

Stacy Curtis is a cartoonist, illustrator,
printmaker, and twin who's illustrated over twenty
children's books, including a *New York Times* best
seller. He and his wife, Jann, live in Oak Lawn,
Illinois, and happily share their home with their dog,
Derby.